Highlights
Hidden Pictures

MAGICAL WOODLAND PUZZLES
Deluxe

Kid Tested by
Aveline Jett
Age 8

See pages
78–88
for crafts,
recipes, and
activities!

HIGHLIGHTS PRESS
Honesdale, Pennsylvania

Magical Playground

umbrella

sock

What's a playground's favorite candy?
Recess pieces.

fried egg

snake

heart

Everyone's having a grand time at this enchanted forest playground. Can you find all the hidden objects in the scene?

kite

screw

lollipop

fish

strawberry

wedge of orange

Art by Katie McDee

3

Night and Day

These images show a daytime and nighttime scene in the same forest. At night, the sky is dark, and the moon is out. Can you find at least 11 other differences between the scenes?

Art by Alexander Jansson

Through the Woods

Princess Petunia loves visiting her woodland friends. Can you find all the hidden objects in this scene?

mitten

comb

bowling pin

ice-cream bar

heart

slice of pie

jump rope

spoon

Art by James Loram

Enchanted Forest Maze

Find the path from START to FINISH.

Gnome Barbershop

This gnome needs a beard trim! Can you find all the hidden objects in the scene?

Art by Kyle Beckett

carrot

golf club

ruler

ladle

safety pin

wedge of lemon

light bulb

lamp

glove

umbrella

leaf

slice of pizza

Six by Six

Each of these small scenes contains **6** hidden objects from the list below. Some objects are hidden in more than one scene. Can you find the **6** hidden objects in each scene?

Hidden Object List

The numbers tell you how many times each object is hidden.

artist's brush (2)
button (3)
carrot (3)
crescent moon (3)
egg (3)
fork (4)
glove (4)
glue bottle (2)
ladder (3)
paper airplane (3)
paper clip (2)
tack (4)

BONUS
Two scenes contain the exact same set of hidden objects. Can you find that matching pair?

Art by Iryna Bodnaruk

9

Magic Creature Patterns

Find the patterns below in the grid.

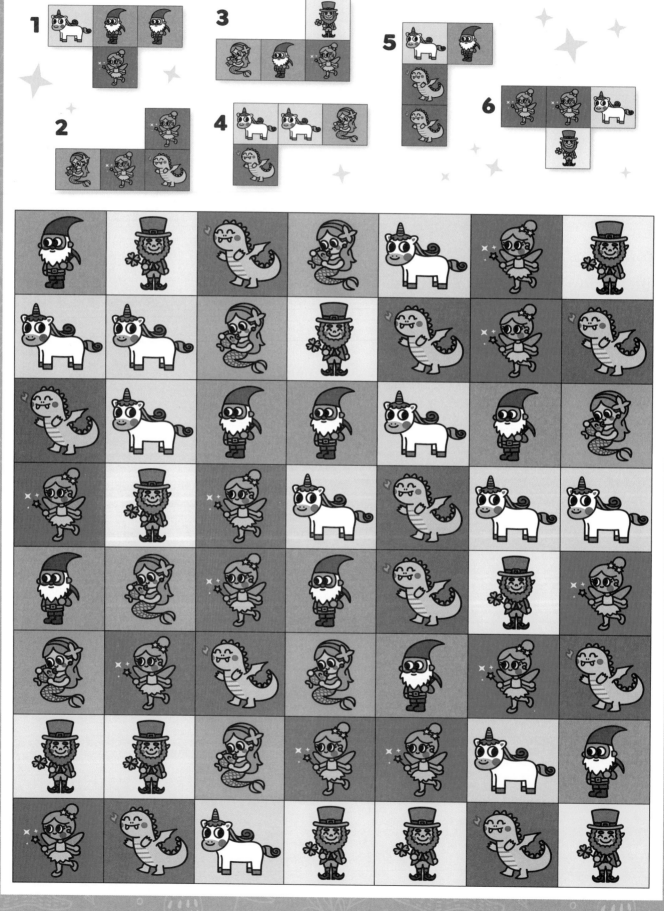

Art by Uijung Kim

Forest Fiddlers

These woodland critters are making spellbinding music! Can you figure out where all the pieces go in the puzzle?

Art by Kristyna Litten

Tic Tac Castle

What do the castles in each row (vertically, horizontally, and diagonally) have in common?

Art by Tim Davis

What kind of cheese surrounds a castle?

Moat-zarella.

What lights does a castle use?

Knight-lights.

12

Unicorn Unicycles

Can you find the hidden bell, crown, eggplant, heart, jump rope, light bulb, paper clip, pencil, piece of popcorn, potato, rainbow, ruler, tack, teacup, thimble, and wedge of lemon?

Art by Letizia Rizzo

13

Food with Friends

key

heart

envelope

glasses

baseball

See if you can find all the hidden objects in the scene before these guests finish their forest dinner party.

Art by Jennifer Naalchigar

broom

star

banana

tack

bowl

muffin

clock

mitten

cutting board

artist's brush

heart

shoe

Sloth Outing

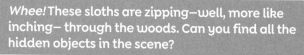

Whee! These sloths are zipping—well, more like inching— through the woods. Can you find all the hidden objects in the scene?

Art by Monika Filipina

fish

pencil

scarf

skateboard

horseshoe

ice-cream bar

banana

teacup

ice-cream cone

spoon

16

Hide it!

Can you hide this mushroom in your own Hidden Pictures drawing?

Art by Gary LaCoste

Unicorn Match

Each of these unicorns has an exact match except one. Can you find the one without a match?

Art by Julissa Mora

Flower Power

Charley the chipmunk has a bouquet of blossoms for his fox friend Farrah. Can you find all the hidden objects in this flowery forest scene?

heart

funnel

crescent moon

arrowhead

yo-yo

artist's brush

boomerang

wishbone

spaceship

toy top

fish

slice of cake

sea star

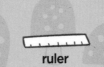
spoon

ruler

glove

Art by Gary Mohrman

19

Tree Talk

Word List

ALDER	CEDAR	HICKORY	OAK	SYCAMORE
APPLE	CHERRY	HOLLY	PALM	WALNUT
ARBORVITAE	CHESTNUT	JUNIPER	PEAR	WILLOW
ASPEN	CYPRESS	LOCUST	PINE	
BEECH	ELM	MAGNOLIA	PLUM	
BIRCH	HACKBERRY	MAPLE	REDWOOD	
BUCKEYE	HEMLOCK	MYRTLE	SPRUCE	

These charmed trees are telling Nancy the knight about different tree types. Can you find the names of 31 kinds of trees in the grid? Look for them up, down, across, backward, and diagonally.

```
                    A
                  E P U
                H E L M T
              G P E U D R V
                H M A
                O A E L L
              L P B Y S O D
            L L B R I H C C E
          Y E O O E G H H W K R
            K R O E Y S O
            C S P R U C E L R
          I M Y R T L E H L E O
        H M C Y P R E S S I D B A
      A S P E N O P I N E W W I W K
        H A C K B E R R Y O R
      M T U N L A W E O Q O C P
    T U N T S E H C Y M E D H V E
  A R B O R V I T A E A R A D E C A
M A G N O L I A S P K C J U N I P E R
          O U P C Y
          S C L U S
          A O E B E
          M L A P R
```

What do you call three trees together?

A tree-o.

How do pine trees like their ice cream?

In a pine cone.

Art by Alexander Jansson

Cottage Puzzler

Which cottage should go in place of each question mark so that each row and column contains all four cottages?

Bears and Bells

These bears are having a blast picnicking in the woods.
See if you can find the 8 bells hidden in the scene.

Art by Emma Latham

Troop of Toadstools

Can you find the gnome?
Can you also find 13 pink flowers?

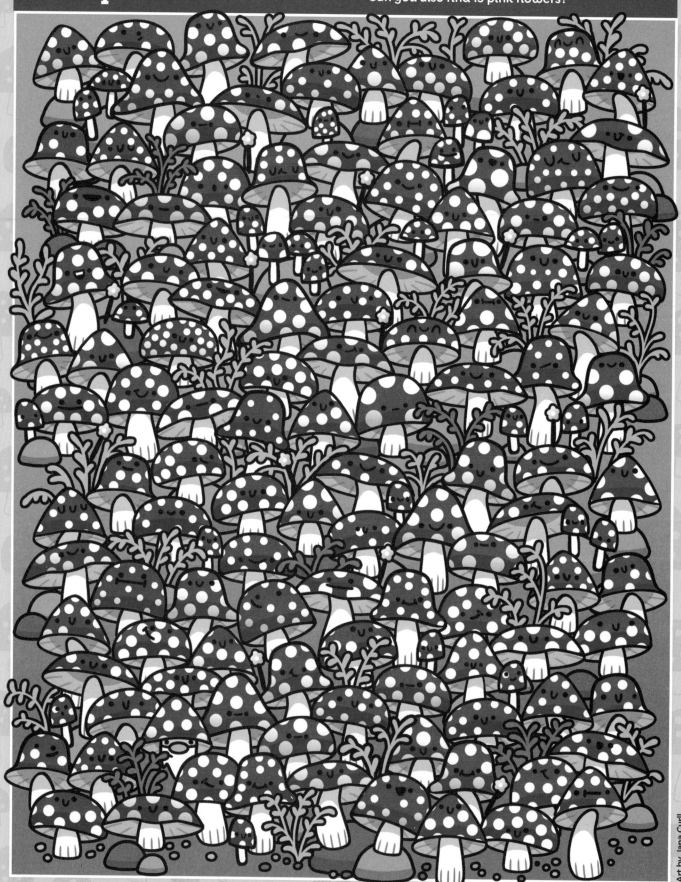

Art by Jana Curll

Draw a Snail

Follow the steps to draw a supercute snail.

1.

2.

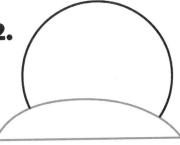

3.

4.

5.

Art by Ron Zalme

Unicorn Wonderland

26

Art by Katie Wood

What lovely music! Can you find at least 12 differences between these two scenes?

What did the guitar say to the singer?

"Stop picking on me!"

Why did the musician need a ladder?

To reach the high notes.

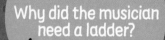

What do you call a musical insect?

A humbug.

What's a frog's favorite song?

"Head, Shoulders, Knees, and Toads."

Movie Night

bowling pin

sailboat

pear

toaster

boomerang

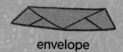
envelope

The audience gives this film five stars!
Can you find all the hidden objects in the scene?

glove

kite

fish

magnifying glass

Art by Josh Cleland

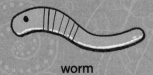

worm

slice of pizza

Marvelous Mushrooms

It's a mushroom meet-up! Can you find all the hidden objects in this scene?

Art by Katie Wood

lollipop

snail shell

paper clip

crown

sand dollar

feather

needle

watermelon wedge

space ship

lime

winter hat

banana

slice of pizza

fidget spinner

ghost

mitten

magic wand

Find the Frogs

Art by Getty Images

Tic Tac Dragon

What do the dragons in each row (vertically, horizontally, and diagonally) have in common?

Art by Kevin Zimmer

What types of stories do dragons tell?

Tall tails.

Why did the dragon cheer?

She was fired up.

34

Welcome Home, Gnome!

Gnorman the gnome is coming home. Can you find all the hidden objects in the scene?

WELCOME HOME GNORMAN!

Art by David Arumi

bowl of popcorn

binoculars

snake

crescent moon

crown

banana

slice of pie

button

envelope

mitten

START

Help this knight find his way through the woods to the magical sword at the end of the path.

FINISH

What is the quietest tool in the garden?

The *shhhovel*.

What did the clothing designer say at her fashion show?

"I'm sew happy!"

Each of these scenes contains 12 hidden objects, which are listed below. Find each object in one of the scenes, then cross it off the list.

artist's brush	domino	heart	ring
battery	doughnut	hockey stick	ruler
boomerang	envelope	horseshoe	slice of pizza
carrot	fishhook	key	tack
comb	football	paper clip	teacup
crescent moon	flag	pencil	waffle

Art by Mitch Mortimer

Fairy Puzzler

Which fairy should go in place of each question mark so that each row and column contains all four fairies?

What do you call a fairy that needs a bath?

Stinkerbell.

What does a fairy like to sing at school?

The elfabet song.

Unicorn Art

These unicorns created a pretty pattern with finds from the forest. Can you find all the hidden objects in this scene?

Art by Gary Mohrman

crescent moon

jester hat

ice-cream cone

spool of thread

pennant

lollipop

magic wand

glove

seashell

wedge of cheese

toothbrush

heart

slice of pie

teacup

whale

lemon

spoon

41

Dragon Wagon

Lucy, her dad, and their dragon are on a stroll. Can you find at least 10 differences between these two scenes? How many times do you see the letter *D* in the scene below?

Why did the dragon eat spicy salsa?

To start the grill.

Try a tongue twister . . .

Say this five times, fast: Dragons drying dripping dishes.

Art by Luke Flowers

Where do you find famous dragons?

In the Hall of Flame.

Try a tongue twister . . .

Say this five times, fast: Dozing dragons dream of diamonds.

Hide-and-Seek

kite

envelope

cane

These forest critters found some good hiding places!
Can you find all the hidden objects in the scene?

fish

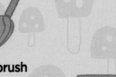

artist's brush

seashell

ruler

pencil

paper clip

"Dibs on the acorns!"

Chalk Art

Aisha and Tamar are decorating the walkway to their treehouse cottage. Can you find all the hidden objects in the scene?

bed

baseball cap

clock

shoe

slice of pizza

pillow

cupcake

chair

Art by Laura Logan

Can you find the knight?
Can you also find 12 gemstones?

Art by Jaka Vukotič

Magical Croquet Match

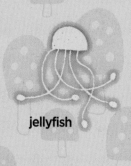
jellyfish

crab

fish

sea star

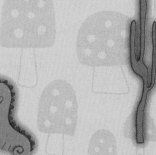
seahorse

seaweed

The centaurs are playing against the gnomes!
Can you find all the hidden objects in the scene?

Art by Ana Zurita

pan flute

comb

squid

puffer fish

clam

seashell

Nighttime Stroll

Vivian greets the nocturnal creatures during her evening walk in the forest. Can you find at least 9 differences between these two scenes?

What did the tree say to the wind?

"Leaf me alone, please!"

Try a tongue twister . . .

Say this five times, fast: The tree tried a tasty treat.

Art by Monika Filipina

Terrific Picnic

Tea, cake, and friends—this picnic has it all!
Can you find all the hidden objects in the scene?

Art by Katie Wood

rocket ship

ice-cream cone

mitten

baseball bat

tack

heart

rainbow

crown

Mushroom Puzzler

Which mushroom should go in place of each question mark so that each row and column contains all four mushrooms?

How does a mushroom clean its house?

With a mush-broom.

What does a mushroom sit on?

A toad-stool.

Each of these small scenes contains **6** hidden objects from the list below. Some objects are hidden in more than one scene. Can you find the **6** hidden objects in each scene?

Hidden Object List

The numbers tell you how many times each object is hidden.

artist's brush (2)
banana (2)
basketball (4)
book (2)
drum (2)
icepop (1)
light bulb (5)
microphone (1)
pencil (4)
shoe (4)
slice of pizza (2)
teacup (3)

BONUS
Two scenes contain the exact same set of hidden objects. Can you find that matching pair?

Art by Luke Flowers

57

Wondrous Woodcarvers

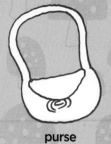

purse

egg

key

balloon

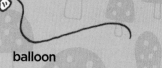

teacup

button

These woodpeckers are carving bears into the tree trunks.
Can you find all the hidden objects in the scene?

comb

fishhook

wishbone

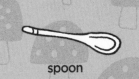
spoon

ring

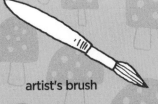
artist's brush

Art by Beccy Blake

Enchanted Taxis

fishhook

ice-cream cone

boot

pants

pencil

crown

envelope

elbow noodle

Need to get somewhere? Hail a dragon taxi!
See if you can find all the hidden objects in the scene.

sailboat

spool of thread

Knock, knock.
Who's there?
Dragon.
Dragon who?
Are you dragon-na let me in?

Art by Kyle Beckett

iron

tent

cupcake

61

Who Knows?
The forest is dark—it's time for night school!
Can you find all the hidden objects in the scene?

chess piece

sailboat

domino

mitten

BONUS!
Can you find
the fishhook,
safety pin,
screwdriver,
necklace,
crescent moon,
drumstick,
and hockey
stick?

Art by Iryna Bodnaruk

comb

fish

trowel

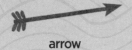
arrow

wedge of orange

ring

Draw a Unicorn

Follow the steps to draw a majestic unicorn.

1.

2.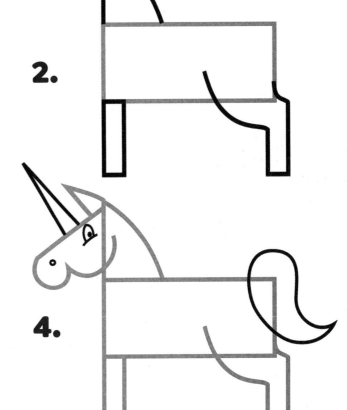

3.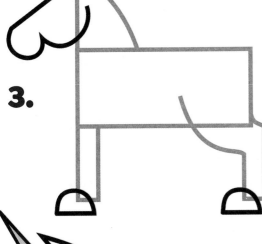

4.

5.

Storytime Fun

banana

cookie

fried egg

heart

toothbrush

piece of
popcorn

crock

slice of pizza

screw

comb

Art by David Arumi

64

Forest Flight

Help the bat find its way through the woods and back to its cave. Use the letters along the path to solve the riddle below.

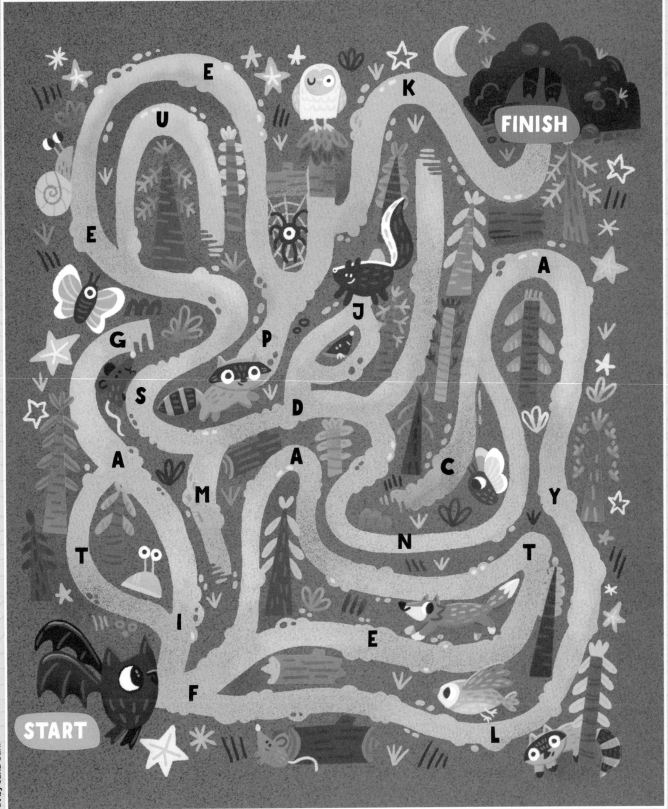

Art by Jana Curll

START

FINISH

What's a bat's favorite game?

_ _ _ - _ _ _ - _ _ _ _ _.

Making Music

What do you call an owl magician?

Whoo-dini.

What runs through the woods without a sound?

A path.

What kind of phone does a turtle use?

A shell phone.

Why did the tree try to make new friends?

It wanted to branch out.

Go with the Flow

While these forest animals raft down the river, can you find all the hidden objects in the scene?

Art by Brian Michael Weaver

toy top

lightning bolt

fork

knitted hat

lollipop

needle

broom

ice-cream bar

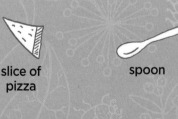
slice of pizza

spoon

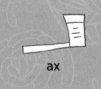
ax

necktie

broccoli

pencil

anchor

comb

magnet

ruler

paper clip

Tic Tac Butterfly

What do the butterflies in each row (vertically, horizontally, and diagonally) have in common?

Art by Carlina Farías

What is a butterfly's favorite subject in school?

Moth-ematics.

What do you call a butterfly's kingdom?

A monarchy.

69

So Many Snails

Can you find the slug? (Hint: Look for the creature without a shell!) Can you also find 12 leaves?

Mushroom Match

Art by Clay Cantrell

Happy Unicorn Day

Art by Ana Zurita

Hootie's All-Night Diner

plunger

crescent
moon

sock

cane

fishhook

whale

baseball
bat

74

Animals come from near and far to eat at Hootie's.
Can you find all the hidden objects in the scene?

balloon

umbrella

glove

pennant

paintbrush

envelope

crayon

A Charmed Drawing

A frog prince, a fairy, and a forest—these unicorns are making an epic drawing! Can you find all the hidden pictures in the scene?

candy cane

spoon

ice-cream cone

broccoli

Art by Paula Bossio

bow tie

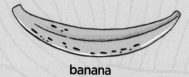

banana

fish

ladder

Cottage Construction

A fairy used magic to build an enchanted cottage. Can you put the images in the correct order?

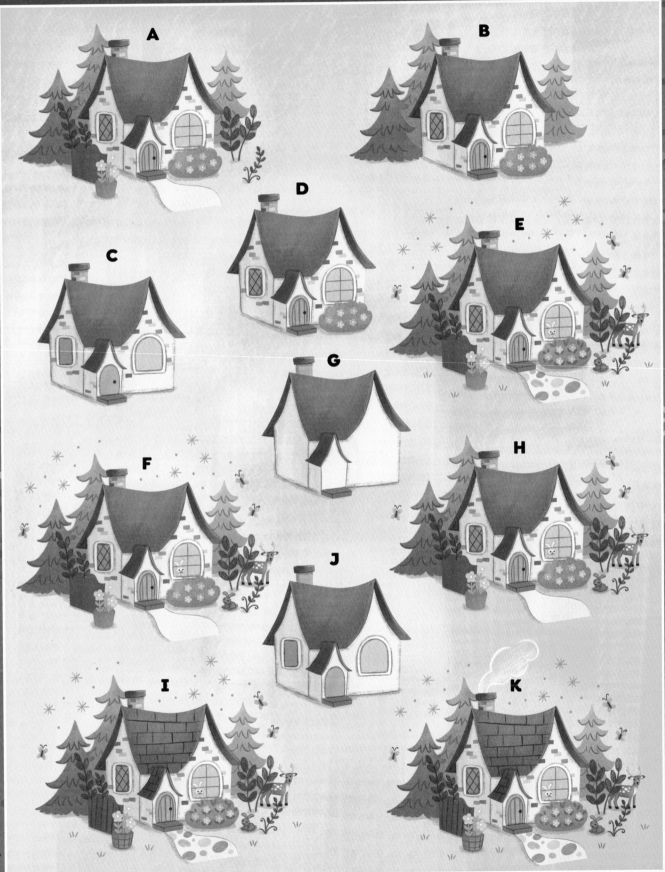

Gnome STONES

Don't forget to make their house!

You Need
* Rocks
* Paints
* Pencil
* Markers

1 Wash a smooth, rounded rock. For a base, paint it white.

2 Use a pencil to draw a gnome's head, a door, or whatever you'd like. Paint it. Use markers to add details.

3 With a parent's OK, put the rocks by a potted plant or near the base of a tree. Avoid putting them where they could damage lawn mowers.

You can say we're rock stars!

Ask an adult before placing painted rocks outside.

Forest Fudge SQUARES

You Need
* Pan
* Parchment paper
* White chocolate chips
* Sweetened condensed milk
* Food coloring
* Metal skewer
* Cereal bits
* Sprinkles

1 Line an 8- or 9-inch pan with parchment paper.

2 Put 16 ounces of white chocolate chips into a microwave-safe bowl.

3 Microwave for 90 seconds at half power. Stir. Add 30 seconds, if necessary.

4 Add 14 ounces of sweetened condensed milk. Stir until smooth.

5 Put the mixture into the pan. Add a few drops of food coloring. Use a metal skewer to swirl it.

6 Top with cereal bits and sprinkles. Chill for 2 hours.

Ask an adult for help with anything hot or sharp.

Pita TREES

You Need
- ★ Pita bread
- ★ Toppings
- ★ Pretzel sticks

Hummus & Olive

Guacamole

Tzatziki & Dill

Cream Cheese & Lox

Nutella & Almonds

 1 Cut a round pita into six or eight sections.

 2 Spread your toppings with the back of a spoon.

 3 Add a pretzel stick to the bottom of the pita to make tree trunk.

Ask an adult for help with anything sharp.

UNICORN Puppet

You Need
- ★ Business envelope (sealed)
- ★ Scissors
- ★ Markers
- ★ Construction Paper
- ★ Tissue Paper
- ★ Double-sided tape
- ★ Pompoms

1 Fold front of the envelope in half. Trim both short ends (to create an opening for your fingers). Fold open ends to middle fold.

2 Draw a horn and two ears on construction paper. Cut them out. Cut tissue paper into long strips.

3 Put double-sided tape on one end of envelope. Press tissue paper strips onto tape.

4 Put tape on the other side of the envelope with tissue paper strips. Add the horn and ears.

5 Put tape over the bottom of the horn and ears. Add pompoms on top. Draw eyes.

Ask an adult for help with anything sharp.

Sock MUSHROOMS

You Need
* Socks
* Scissors
* Polyester fiberfill
* String
* Low-temperature glue gun
* Tacky glue
* Decorations like pompons and felt

1 For the top of each mushroom, cut off the toe of a sock. For the stem, cut off the heel and leg cuff of a sock. Stuff each with polyester fiberfill.

2 Use pieces of string to tie both the mushroom top and the stem closed. (Secure them with glue if you'd like.)

3 Trim the string and any extra sock fabric.

Cut leaves from colorful felt!

4 Use a low-temperature glue gun to connect the top of each mushroom to its stem.

5 Use tacky glue to attach decorations to each mushroom top.

Ask an adult before choosing socks to use. Ask an adult for help with anything hot or sharp.

Make Your Own Trail Mix

> Visiting an enchanted (or regular) forest? Bring a snack!

You Need
* Variety of snacks
* Plastic container

1 Add at least one ingredient from each category into the container.

2 Shake to mix.

Crunchy Munchies

 pita chips

pretzels

popcorn

cereal

Fruity Nibbles

 dried cranberries

 dried apple slices

fruit gummies

banana chips

Protein Packers

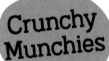 mixed nuts

pumpkin seeds

roasted chickpeas

granola clusters

Sweet Surprises

 animal crackers

 yogurt-covered raisins

 mini marshmallows

  chocolate chips

Flavor Blasts

Spicy!

 wasabi peas

sesame rice sticks

 peanut-butter chips

 flavored jerky

Breadstick WANDS

You Need
* Refrigerated pizza dough
* Baking sheet
* Egg
* Water
* Paper towel
* Sprinkles

1 *Adult:* preheat the oven to 425°F. Unroll the dough.

2 Cut the dough into thin strips. Place the strips onto greased baking sheet.

3 Whisk one egg with water. Dip the paper towel into the mixture and dab onto dough.

4 Decorate your dough! *Adult:* bake the breadsticks for 9–10 minutes until golden brown and shiny.

↶ Step 1

↶ Step 2

↶ Step 3

Ask an adult for help with anything sharp.

Build a CASTLE

You Need
★ Scissors
★ Cardboard tubes
★ Cardstock
★ Tacky glue
★ Markers

Make flags out of toothpicks and cardstock!

1 Trim cardboard tubes to different sizes. Cut slits in the bottom of each tube and cut out rectangular notches from the top.

2 Use a black marker to draw on windows and doors.

3 Make two roofs by twisting two pieces of cardstock into cones. Use tacky glue to attach each roof to one end of a tube.

4 Stack the cardboard tubes together to make a castle.

Ask an adult for help with anything sharp.

KNIGHT LIGHT

You Need
* Glue
* Cardstock
* Scissors
* Oatmeal container
* Scrapbook paper
* Metal fasteners
* Fuzzy sticks
* Wiggle eyes
* Colored tape
* Battery-powered light

Turn on the light to make it glow!

1 Glue cardstock onto an empty oatmeal container. Cut a hole in the center.

2 From scrapbook paper, cut out a face shield.

3 Use metal fasteners to attach the shield to the container.

4 Coil two fuzzy sticks. Glue a wiggle eye on each. Tape them inside the container.

5 Add colored tape and a cardstock plume to the knight. Place a battery-powered light inside.

Ask an adult for help with anything sharp.

UNICORN Popcorn

Add a magical twist to this classic movie snack.

1 *Adult:* pop some popcorn.

2 Place the marshmallows, sprinkles, and pudding mix into a bag with the popcorn, then shake.

3 If needed, use butter spray to help the pudding mix stick.

4 Pour the mixture into a bowl.

You Need
- ★ Popcorn
- ★ Marshmallows
- ★ Sprinkles
- ★ Pudding mix
- ★ Butter spray (optional)

marshmallows

sprinkles

pudding mix

SEED BALLS

Forests are home to pretty flowers. Grow your own blossoms with these seed balls!

1 Tear scraps of construction paper into tiny pieces. Place them in a heat-safe bowl.

2 *Adult:* Boil water. Pour it over the paper pieces, covering them completely. Let it sit for 2–3 minutes.

3 Mash the mixture with a spoon. Mix for 15 seconds. Repeat until it is a thick paste.

4 Using a sieve or a paper towel, drain or squeeze the excess water from the paper pulp.

5 Add flower seeds to the pulp. (If the seeds need to be spaced out when planting, use only one seed per ball.)

6 Form the pulp into balls (about golf-ball size). Plant them in soil in a pot. Water them, and watch the flowers grow!

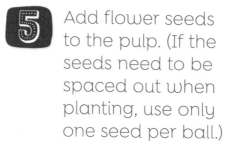

Answers

▼ Pages 2–3

▼ Page 4

▼ Page 5

▼ Page 6

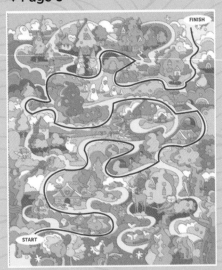

▼ Page 7

▼ Pages 8–9

▼ Page 10

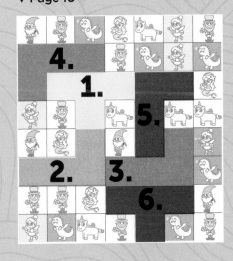

Answers

▼ Page 11

1. D
2. E
3. C
4. G
5. H
6. A
7. B
8. F

▼ Page 12

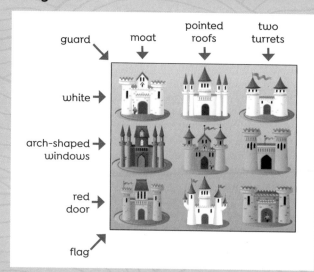

▼ Page 13

▼ Pages 14–15

▼ Page 16

▼ Page 18

▼ Page 19

▼ Pages 20–21

Answers

▼ Page 22

▼ Page 23

▼ Page 24

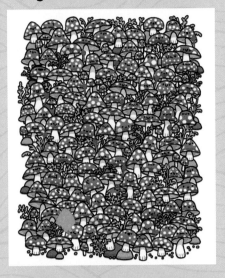

▼ Pages 26–27

▼ Pages 28–29

▼ Pages 30–31

▼ Page 32

Answers

▼ Page 33

▼ Page 34

Purple feet Tail spikes Yellow eyes	**Purple feet** Tail fin	**Purple feet Teeth** Yellow wings
Nose horns Tail spikes	Nose horns **Tail fin** Yellow eyes Yellow wings	Nose horns **Teeth**
Polka dots Yellow wings Tail spikes	**Polka dots** Tail fin	**Polka dots Teeth** Yellow eyes

▼ Page 35

▼ Pages 36–37

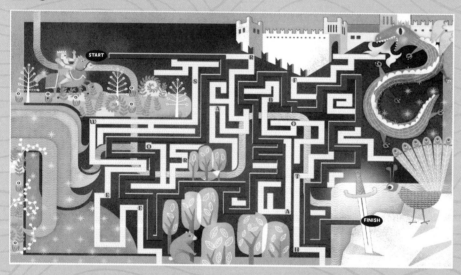

▼ Pages 38–39

▼ Page 40

Answers

▼ Page 41

▼ Pages 42-43

The letter *D* appears 6 times in the scene.

▼ Pages 44-45

▼ Pages 46-47

▼ Page 48

Answers

▼ Page 49

▼ Pages 50–51

▼ Pages 52–53

▼ Page 54

▼ Page 55

▼ Pages 56–57

Answers

▼ Pages 58–59

▼ Pages 60–61

▼ Page 62

▼ Page 64

▼ Page 65

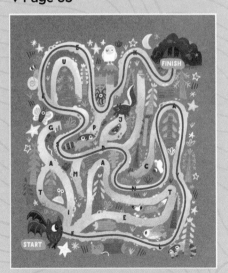

▼ Page 66–67

RIDDLE ANSWER: FLY-AND-SEEK.

95

Answers

▼ **Page 68**

▼ **Page 69**

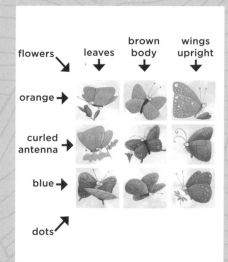

▼ **Page 70**

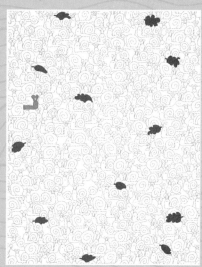

▼ **Page 71**

▼ **Pages 72–73**

1. F
2. G
3. A
4. E
5. H
6. J
7. I
8. D
9. B
10. C

▼ **Pages 74–75**

▼ **Page 76**

▼ **Page 77**

1. G
2. J
3. C
4. D
5. B
6. A
7. H
8. F
9. I
10. K

For information about permission to reprint selections from this book, please contact permissions@highlights.com.
Published by Highlights Press
815 Church Street
Honesdale, Pennsylvania 18431
ISBN: 978-1-63962-254-2
Manufactured in Shenzhen, Guangdong, China
Mfg. 04/2024
First edition
Visit our website at Highlights.com.
10 9 8 7 6 5 4 3 2 1
Cover art by Katie Wood
Craft and recipe photos by Jim Filipski, Guy Cali Associates, Inc., except for Pita Trees (p. 80) and Make Your Own Trail Mix (p. 83) by Rich Brainerd Studios, Sock Mushrooms (p. 82) by Ashley Toth, Castle (p. 85) by Jodi Levine, Unicorn Popcorn (p. 87) by Alexandra Grablewski, Seed Balls (p. 88) by Thomas Michael Lowery
2254-01

Create Your Own Mushroom Fairy Village! Color in the different drawings, and then cut them out. You can make stands for the trees, cottages, and other parts of the village so they stay upright. To make stands, cut triangles from cardstock. Fold one side of each triangle to create a tab. Tape or glue the tab of each triangle to the back of a village part. Ask an adult for help with anything sharp.

Stand Examples:

Make one stand. **OR** Make two smaller stands for extra support.

Tape or glue →

Fold